TRAVEL WITH THE GREAT EXPLORERS

Explore with

Samuel de Champlain

Cynthia O'Brien

Crabtree Publishing Company

www.crabtreebooks.com

Crabtree Publishing Company

www.crabtreebooks.com

Author: Cynthia O'Brien
Publishing plan research and development:
   Reagan Miller
Managing editor: Tim Cooke
Editorial director: Lindsey Lowe
Editors: Kelly Spence, Natalie Hyde
Proofreader: Crystal Sikkens
Designer: Lynne Lennon
Picture manager: Sophie Mortimer
Design manager: Keith Davis
Children's publisher: Anne O'Daly
Production coordinator
   and prepress technican: Tammy McGarr
Print coordinator: Margaret Amy Salter

Produced by Brown Bear Books for
   Crabtree Publishing Company.

Photographs:
Front Cover:
Alamy: Interfoto main; **Corbis**: tr; **istockphoto**: cr;
Shutterstock: br.

Interior:
Alamy: Interfoto 8bl, North Wind Picture Archives 6, 7t, 17,
21t, 24tr, 25b, 29t, Timewatch Images 16b: **Bridgeman Art
Library**: Private Collection 9, 28; **Corbis**: 25t, The Mariners
Museum 19; **Dreamstime**: 13br; **istockphoto**: 7b. 16tr. 26cl, 26-
27; **Mary Evans Picture Library**: 12t, 13c, 26bl; Grenville
Collins Postcard Collection 20; Grosvenor Prints 15bl; **North
Wind Picture Archives**: 10-11; **Public Domain**: 18, Myrabella 8-
9; **Shutterstock**: 12b, 22t, 28-29: **Thinkstock**: istockphoto 22b,
23; **Topfoto**: Fotomas 15t, Image Works 10, Liszt Collecton
21b, The Granger Collection 11, 14,
24bl, 27tl:

Library and Archives Canada Cataloguing in Publication

O'Brien, Cynthia (Cynthia J.), author
      Explore with Samuel de Champlain / Cynthia O'Brien.

(Travel with the great explorers)
Includes index.
Issued in print and electronic formats.
ISBN 978-0-7787-1256-5 (bound).--ISBN 978-0-7787-1260-2 (pbk.).--
ISBN 978-1-4271-7575-5 (pdf).--ISBN 978-1-4271-7571-7 (html)

      1. Champlain, Samuel de, 1567-1635--Juvenile literature.
2. Explorers--Canada--Biography--Juvenile literature. 3. Explorers--
France--Biography--Juvenile literature. 4. Canada--Discovery and
exploration--French--Juvenile literature. 5. Canada--History--To
1663 (New France)--Juvenile literature. I. Title.

FC332.O37 2014   j971.01'13092   C2013-908707-9
                                                                            C2013-908708-7

Library of Congress Cataloging-in-Publication Data

O'Brien, Cynthia (Cynthia J.)
   Explore with Samuel de Champlain / Cynthia O'Brien.
      pages cm. -- (Travel with the great explorers)
   Includes index.
   ISBN 978-0-7787-1256-5 (reinforced library binding) -- ISBN 978-0-
7787-1260-2 (pbk.) -- ISBN 978-1-4271-7575-5 (electronic pdf) -- ISBN
978-1-4271-7571-7 (electronic html)
1. Champlain, Samuel de, 1574-1635--Juvenile literature. 2. America--
Discovery and exploration--French--Juvenile literature. 3. New France--
Discovery and exploration--Juvenile literature. 4. Explorers--America--
Biography--Juvenile literature. 5. Explorers--France--Biography--
Juvenile literature. I. Title.

F1030.1.O37 2014
910.92'2--dc23
[B]
                                          2013050840

Crabtree Publishing Company

www.crabtreebooks.com 1-800-387-7650

Printed in Canada/022014/MA20131220

Published in Canada
Crabtree Publishing
616 Welland Ave.
St. Catharines, ON
L2M 5V6

Published in the United States
Crabtree Publishing
PMB 59051
350 Fifth Avenue, 59th Floor
New York, New York 10118

Published in the United Kingdom
Crabtree Publishing
Maritime House
Basin Road North, Hove
BN41 1WR

Published in Australia
Crabtree Publishing
3 Charles Street
Coburg North
VIC, 3058

CONTENTS

Meet the Boss

Who was Samuel de Champlain? There are no true portraits of the explorer. There are no birth records. However, Champlain's later writings and other documents provide clues to his early life.

MYSTERY SOLVED?

+ Old document found in France

Historians have puzzled over Champlain's birthdate for centuries. Finally, in spring 2012, a French **genealogist** uncovered an important clue. An old **baptism** record stated that a son, Samuel, was born to Anthoynee Chapeleau and Margerite Le Roy on Friday, August 13, 1574. It also states that the family was Huguenot, or Protestant. Was Champlain born Protestant? Is this his baptismal record? The slight difference in the name makes it impossible to be sure.

IT'S IN THE BLOOD

☛ **Father passes on knowledge of seafaring**

☛ **Champlain goes to sea as a child**

Champlain was born near the ocean, in the French town of Brouage. His father was a captain in the French navy, and Champlain went to sea as a young boy. Learning from his father, he became a skillful **pilot**. When he was older, Champlain wrote, "This art it is which from my tender youth won my love, has stimulated me to venture nearly all my life upon the turbulent waves of the ocean."

THE KING'S MAN

★ Ruler Helps Explorer's Family

In 1589, King Henry IV came to the French throne. He ended a long war between Catholics and Protestants in France. Although Henry became Catholic when he became king, he was originally a Protestant, most likely the same as Champlain's family. The king helped Champlain, who served in his army from about 1594 to 1598. He may have acted as a spy for Henry. Later, Champlain became one of the royal geographers.

> "To Samuel de Champlain, the sum of nine ecus for a certain secret voyage in which he has made an important service to the king."
> *Record of government payment to Champlain*

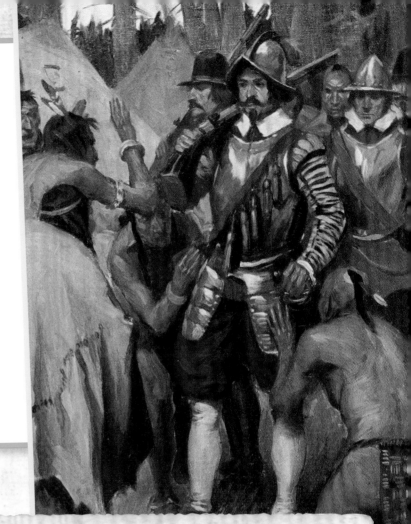

LET'S SHAKE HANDS

+ Champlain seeks tolerance and peace

+ Earns trust of First Nations

Champlain learned a lot from his experiences as a soldier. Later his reports on his Caribbean travels told of Spanish cruelty toward native people. Champlain was outraged. He believed in respectful, peaceful relationships with all people. This was an unusual attitude at the time. When Champlain traveled to North America, he gained the trust of the First Nations people he met. In turn, they became trustworthy trading partners, guides, and friends.

Did you know?

Champlain came from the French port of Brouage. In the 17th century the town's harbor silted up, or filled with sand and clay. The port ceased to exist and the town fell into ruin.

Where Are We Heading?

Samuel de Champlain was an explorer, mapmaker, and governor. He explored what is now eastern Canada for the French. He earned the title "Father of New France," for the colony he helped establish.

FIRST IMPRESSIONS

- Royal geographer travels to New France
- Reaches the Lachine Rapids

In March 1603, Champlain made his first trip to New France. French explorers had already sailed up the Saint Lawrence River. Champlain explored the Saguenay River as far as the Lachine Rapids. First Nations guides told him about the territory that lay beyond.

Weather Forecast

HEAVY SNOW TO COME

In June 1604, Champlain and Pierre Dugua, Sieur de Mons, arrived in Acadia, the French colony in what is now Nova Scotia. On St. Croix Island, they built a small settlement. As winter began, fresh food ran out. Almost half of the 79 settlers died of scurvy or other illnesses.

A ROYAL COLONY

★ **French trader chooses new site**

★ **Avoids earlier mistakes**

When the colony at St. Croix failed, Champlain and de Mons looked for a better spot to settle. Port Royal, on the Bay of Fundy, was well-protected and **fertile**. The settlers built shelters and planted gardens. Champlain explored and mapped the coastline.

TRAVEL UPDATE

New path to the Orient?

★ If you're heading out on a journey, make sure you know how far you are going. Champlain hoped to find a shortcut from New France to China. He had no idea that Canada was so big. In 1613, Champlain traveled west on the Ottawa River looking for China, but gave up at Morrison Island, near the modern-day Ontario/Quebec border.

Passage

Europeans hoped a "northwest passage" led around or through America to Asia. The route would make it easier to trade spices and other goods.

LOCATION, LOCATION!

Champlain founded Quebec City in the summer of 1608. The following winter, he stayed in the new settlement with 28 other men. By the spring, only nine men had survived, including Champlain himself.

I NAME THIS LAKE "CHAMPLAIN"

☛ **Expedition goes south**

In July 1609, Champlain again ventured beyond Quebec. This time, he and his First Nations' guides traveled south along the Iroquois River (now the Richelieu). They arrived at a long, narrow lake in Maine, which the French explorer named Lake Champlain. This was the site of Champlain's first battle with the Mohawks.

CHAMPLAIN'S EXPLORATIONS IN NORTH AMERICA

The French explorer first visited North America in 1604, when he explored Nova Scotia and the Saint Lawrence River. On two later journeys shown here, he explored a large area of what would become Canada.

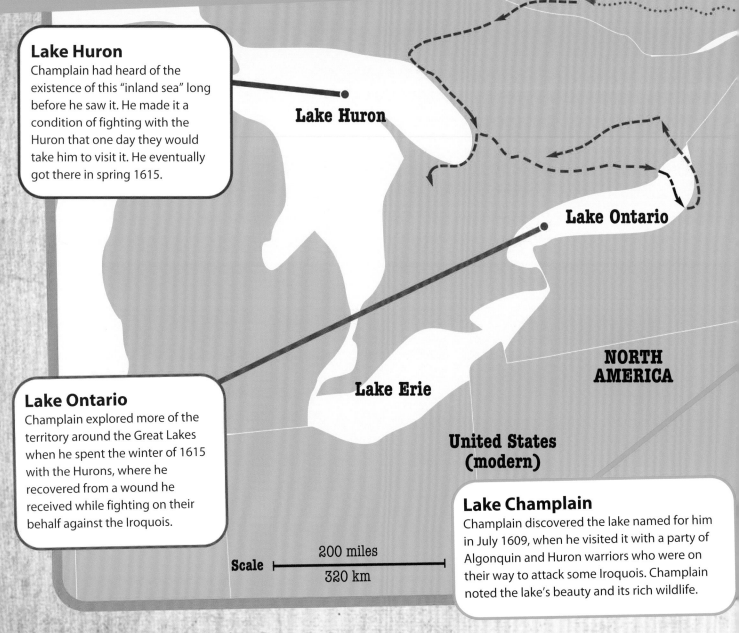

Lake Huron
Champlain had heard of the existence of this "inland sea" long before he saw it. He made it a condition of fighting with the Huron that one day they would take him to visit it. He eventually got there in spring 1615.

Lake Huron

Lake Ontario

NORTH AMERICA

Lake Erie

United States (modern)

Lake Ontario
Champlain explored more of the territory around the Great Lakes when he spent the winter of 1615 with the Hurons, where he recovered from a wound he received while fighting on their behalf against the Iroquois.

Scale | 200 miles / 320 km |

Lake Champlain
Champlain discovered the lake named for him in July 1609, when he visited it with a party of Algonquin and Huron warriors who were on their way to attack some Iroquois. Champlain noted the lake's beauty and its rich wildlife.

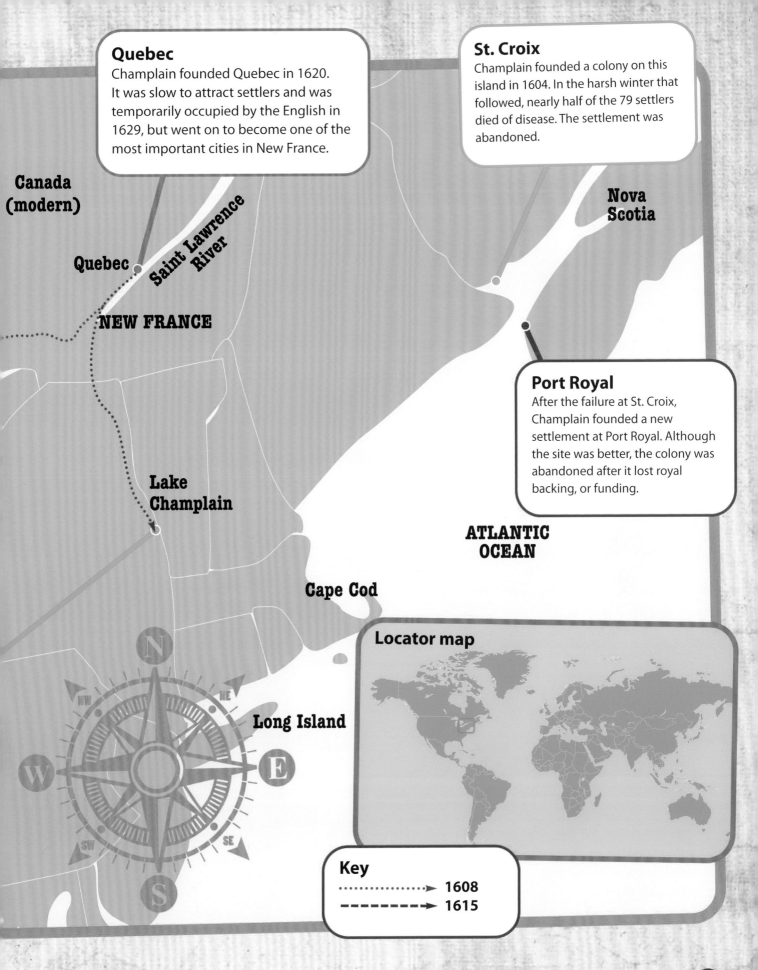

Quebec
Champlain founded Quebec in 1620. It was slow to attract settlers and was temporarily occupied by the English in 1629, but went on to become one of the most important cities in New France.

St. Croix
Champlain founded a colony on this island in 1604. In the harsh winter that followed, nearly half of the 79 settlers died of disease. The settlement was abandoned.

Canada (modern)

Quebec

Saint Lawrence River

Nova Scotia

NEW FRANCE

Port Royal
After the failure at St. Croix, Champlain founded a new settlement at Port Royal. Although the site was better, the colony was abandoned after it lost royal backing, or funding.

Lake Champlain

ATLANTIC OCEAN

Cape Cod

Locator map

N
NW   NE
W   E
SW   SE
S

Long Island

Key
·············▶ 1608
- - - - - -▶ 1615

Meet the Crew

King Henry IV appreciated Samuel de Champlain's talents. With the king's favor, the young Frenchman met other people who would help his ambition to explore.

Mover and Shaker

☞ **Nobleman helps found settlement**

☞ **Wants to get into the fur trade**

Pierre Dugua, Sieur de Mons, was a French nobleman. In 1603, Henry IV granted him a fur trade **monopoly**, or control, in the french colony, Acadia. In exchange, Dugua de Mons agreed to found colonies and convert the Aboriginal people to Christianity. In 1604, Champlain traveled with Dugua de Mons to New France. Dugua de Mons founded the settlements of St. Croix and Port Royal. Other investors broke his monopoly on trading in furs, however, and Dugua de Mons' role in New Canada ended.

> " The Sieur de Mons asked if I would agree to make this voyage with him."
> *Champlain on his invitation to Canada*

MASTER TRANSLATOR

Very little is known about Mathieu da Costa, the first African man to visit Canada. Skilled in languages, da Costa probably spoke Dutch, Spanish, and French. In addition, he learned to speak Algonquin and Mi'kmaq **dialects**. Sieur de Mons hired da Costa as a translator, and it is likely that he helped Champlain at some point.

FATHER FIGURE

★ **Captain takes mapmaker under his wing**

★ **Pont-Gravé leads settlements**

Champlain had great respect for Francois Gravé, Sieur du Pont. Pont-Gravé, as he was known, was an experienced seaman and fur trader. He set up a trading post at Tadoussac in 1599 and later commanded Port Royal. Pont-Gravé commanded the ship, *Don-de-Dieu*, during Champlain's first voyage to New France.

My Explorer Journal

★ **The early colonists in New France faced great hardship. They needed determination and skills to survive. Use details from the book to write a letter to Champlain. Explain why you want to be a colonist and what skills you possess.**

BUILDERS OF THE NEW FRANCE

+ **Wanted: strong, brave men**

All of the first settlers in New France were men. Most were soldiers and laborers. Some were teenage boys. They needed to be good at building, at farming, and at hunting for food. They had to be physically strong to cope with the work. They also had to be able to live without luxuries, as life was very basic. Women only moved to the colonies much later.

Brulé

One teenage settler, Etienne Brulé, became an explorer himself. Champlain arranged for him to live among the First Nations people.

Check Out the Ride

Large ships took traders and explorers from Europe to the New World. Once there, Champlain needed other options for travel.

"A Good Sailor"

- ☞ Royal cartographer joins Spanish crew
- ☞ Visits Caribbean, South America

Champlain's first major trip was aboard the *Saint Julien* in 1599. It was an old *naivre*, or merchant ship. This 500-ton (454-metric ton) vessel took him first to Spain and then to the Spanish colonies. He visited Puerto Rico, Mexico, Panama, and Cuba.

> "To make inquiries into particulars of which no Frenchman had been able to gain knowledge."
> *Samuel de Champlain explains why he visited Spain.*

CAPTAIN OF THE SHIP

+ Champlain takes charge on new expedition

In 1604, de Mons crossed the Atlantic Ocean on the 150-ton (136-metric ton) ship, *Don-de-Dieu*, meaning Gift of God. Champlain, the royal **cartographer**, was onboard. In 1608, Champlain got his chance to take charge. He set sail from France in April and arrived in Tadoussac two months later.

Working Boats

- Right size for the job
- Variety of boats

Large ships carried smaller vessels for use in New France and Acadia, including **barques**, **shallops**, and skiffs, or smaller boats. Champlain used all three, but for different purposes. Barques and shallops carried building materials and supplies. For charting protected harbors, Champlain used small skiffs.

A CLOSER LOOK

- ★ Explorer braves coastal rocks
- ★ Maps the coastline

One of Champlain's favorite boats was a **patache**. This shallow, light boat could be steered close to shore and was ideal for exploring rugged coastlines. Champlain called this kind of exploration "ferreting," and he loved to do it. He made detailed maps and sketches of the Atlantic coast with this method. Inland, Champlain used river barques for ferreting. He sketched and made notes of what he saw and often went ashore to collect samples of soil and plants.

Did you know?

Champlain's maps of New France were some of the most accurate maps of modern Canada produced for over a century.

TRAVEL UPDATE

In the Wilderness

★Champlain learned how to travel in the wilderness from the First Nations. Their birchbark canoes were strong, but light enough to carry. Carrying a boat over land is called a **portage**. Champlain portaged with his First Nations guides in New France.

Solve It With Science

As an explorer and cartographer, Champlain relied heavily on science. He navigated the oceans and mapped the land using astronomy, math, charts, and instruments.

WHERE ARE WE?

- Navigating with the stars
- Long-lost mystery

Champlain used a number of instruments for navigating and mapping. These included a compass, telescope, and **cross-staff**. However, the instrument most famously associated with Champlain is the **astrolabe**. Explorers used the astrolabe to determine a ship's **latitude** and direction. It relied on the position of the Sun, Moon, and stars. In 1867, a teenager named Edward Lee was helping his father to clear some trees in an area northwest of Ottawa. There he uncovered an astrolabe. It was the right age and in the right place to be Champlain's lost astrolabe. No one will ever know for sure, but it was a great find.

TRAVEL UPDATE

Mapping it

★Mapping a new land is a great challenge. To begin with, you need to study. Champlain likely learned cartography while working at the Louvre with other royal geographers and cartographers. It's also useful to consult experienced sailors and travelers, again like Champlain. From detailed notes, calculations, and drawings, he created amazingly accurate maps. He also relied on the great knowledge of the First Nations people. The explorer's map of New France, published in 1632, is a masterpiece of cartography.

Settling

Champlain's maps helped France settle new territories by showing what the land could offer.

READY, AIM, FIRE!

★ Smoking gun

In the early 1600s, French soldiers used portable guns called arquebuses. This long-barreled, wheel-lock gun fired when the wheel turned against a piece of metal, igniting the gunpowder. First Nations warriors, who carried spears, bows, and arrows, could not compete against the firepower of the arquebus. Soldiers needed experience and skill to handle a gun well. Champlain and his men had both.

Hanging at Home

Forget about being comfortable. For the early settlers who followed Champlain to New France, life was full of hard work and challenges. There was little time to relax.

TRAVEL UPDATE

Are we there yet?

★Sailing across the ocean from France to North America takes many weeks. In the past, ships were loaded with food supplies: salted meat and fish, sacks of grain, water, wine, dried fruit and vegetables, and even live animals. In addition, the ship carried materials, such as wood, for building shelters.

> Several of our men had their faces so swollen by mosquito bites that they could scarcely see."
> *Champlain on life on St. Croix island*

🌧️ Weather Forecast

WINTER SUFFERING

At first, St. Croix looked like an ideal place to settle in the summer of 1604. It was a tree-covered island at the mouth of what is now the St. Croix River. Champlain drew a plan of the settlement. But the island had poor soil and little fresh water. That winter, the settlers had little fresh food. Almost half of them died of scurvy or other illnesses.

THE ORDER OF GOOD CHEER

+ Let's party

Winters were long and cold in Acadia. Champlain and his friend, Jean de Biencourt, Sieur de Poutrincourt, came up with an idea to prevent the settlers from becoming too depressed. They began a social club called The Order of Good Cheer. The colonists took turns hosting a party, laying out fabulous feasts, and arranging entertainment for their guests. Membertou, the Mi'kmaq chief, often came to these parties. The club boosted the spirits of the settlers and brought people together.

A TROUBLED COLONY

- De Mons seeks funds
- Port Royal temporarily abandoned

In 1605, Champlain's friend, Pierre Dugua, Sieur du Mons, returned to France to find more money for the new colony at Port Royal. This did not happen, so the king ordered the settlers return to France in 1607. Chief Membertou looked after the settlement for three years, until the French noble de Poutrincourt returned to establish a new trading post. Just three years later, the English attacked and destroyed Port Royal.

Quebec!

Champlain visited Quebec in 1603. When he returned in 1608, he founded a settlement. It became the most important town in New France.

My Explorer Journal

★ **The Order of Good Cheer held regular feasts to keep everyone's spirits high. Plan your own menu for a feast in New France. Read on to find details in the text to help you. Explain the kinds of entertainment that might be available.**

FAMILY LIFE

★ **Explorer marries young Parisian**

In Paris in 1610, Champlain married a young girl, Hélène Boullé. Only 12 years old at the time, Hélène joined her husband in Quebec in 1620, but went to France after four years. She never returned to Quebec.

Meeting and Greeting

Champlain's relationship with the Huron and Algonquin First Nations was crucial to his success in New France. They offered help, knowledge, and friendship.

First Encounters

- Observing and learning
- Explorer uses native guides

Champlain first met North American people when he traveled to the Spanish colonies. He found them fascinating, and his interest in aboriginal cultures continued. Champlain realized that he could learn a lot from First Nations people, and he sought their advice on his very first trip to New France. He asked them to draw what they knew of the land using charcoal and white birch bark. From these drawings and their stories, Champlain gained knowledge of the country far north and west of the Saint Lawrence River.

GRAND CHIEF

- ★ Mi'kmaq welcome French
- ★ First Christian convert

The Mi'kmaq grand chief, Membertou, welcomed the French when they settled in Port Royal. Father Biard, a Jesuit priest, wrote, "This was the greatest, most renowned and most formidable [native person] within the memory of man." In June 1610, Membertou became the first Native Canadian to be baptized in New France.

Did you know?

In 1628, Champlain adopted three Montagnais girls as his daughters. He named them Faith, Hope, and Charity.

> "All these people are of a joyous humor, and they laugh frequently."
>
> *Champlain describes the Algonquin.*

PARTY HARD

+ Hundreds of guests attend party

The *tabagie* was a traditional Algonquin celebration. Champlain first joined a *tabagie* in 1603, where he met Anadabijou and Tassoüat, the Algonquin chiefs. The celebration was in honor of a victory over the Iroquois. Hundreds of people attended the party. They feasted on bear, elk, seal, and beaver, and there was dancing and singing. This first French–First Nations *tabagie* was a sign of the new friendship between the two cultures.

Weather Forecast

YEAR-ROUND HOME

The first Algonquin people Champlain met were Kitcisipiriniwak, who lived on the Ottawa River. Unlike other Algonquin, the Kitcisipiriniwak did not move to other locations as the seasons changed. Winters were cold, with heavy snowfall, but a little milder than in other places.

Friends and Enemies

Champlain spent more time working and living with First Nations people than most other explorers. He learned from them and even fought alongside them.

WORKING TOGETHER

+ Special partnerships form

+ What's in a name?

Champlain called the first people he met in New France Montagnais. This means "mountain dwellers" in French. The Montagnais, today called Innu, were important trading partners. They were great hunters and provided the French with a lot of fur. They also introduced Champlain to his First Nations allies, the Algonquins and Hurons. These names are French, as well. Today, the Algonquins are called Anishnabe, meaning "original person," and the Hurons are Wendat, meaning "islanders."

Who were the Iroquois?

☞ Champlain fights powerful Confederacy

The Iroquois Confederacy included five nations: the Oneida, Mohawk, Onondaga, Cayuga, and Seneca. By the time Champlain arrived in New France, the war between the Iroquois and their northern neighbors had been raging for many years. Champlain sided with the enemies of the Iroquois.

> " These people sometimes suffer great extremity, on account of the great cold and snow."
> *Samuel de Champlain on First Nations people*

NATIONS AT WAR

★ **Champlain aids First Nation allies**

★ **Explorer fires fatal shots**

In July 1609, Champlain agreed to fight with the Montagnais, Algonquin, and Huron against some Iroquois, including some Mohawk. He and two French soldiers joined the warriors and traveled to Lake Champlain. They found a Mohawk camp. At dawn, Champlain and his allies attacked. The French soldiers killed two Mohawk chiefs with their arquebuses and wounded another. Shocked by the guns, the other Mohawk fled. In 1610, Champlain fought in another battle that drove the Iroquois Confederacy from the lower St. Lawrence Valley.

(quill illustration)

My Explorer Journal

★ **Imagine you are an Iroquois warrior. Describe how it might have felt to face gunpowder weapons for the first time in the shape of Champlain's arquebus.**

Wounded

Fighting the Oneida in 1615, Champlain said that arrows "fell upon us like hail." He was hit in his leg and knee, and was badly wounded.

Life Among the Hurons

☛ **Allies in war and peace**

☛ **Wounded in battle**

In 1615, the Iroquois presented a new threat. This time, Champlain and hundreds of Huron warriors traveled south of Lake Ontario to an Oneida village. The Oneida wounded Champlain and the Hurons carried him back to Ontario. Champlain spent the winter there, meeting neighboring tribes such as the Nipissing.

I Love Nature

The first farms in New France and Acadia used seeds brought from France. They grew vegetables and grains.

TIMBER!

- Settlers clear land for crops
- Milling technology arrives in America

One of the first jobs in a new settlement was cutting down trees. This made room for planting crops. For the French, one of the most important crops was wheat. Bread was a staple food at all meals. After growing the wheat, the settlers needed to grind it for flour. In 1606, the colonists at Port Royal built a water-driven gristmill that was likely the first in North America. In Quebec, Champlain had his own garden and encouraged the other settlers to do the same.

TRAVEL UPDATE

What's on the Menu?

★ In a new settlement most meals were basic: soup, fish, and bread. Growing your own vegetables helped to add variety. According to Champlain "the gardens contained all kinds of plants, cabbages, radishes, lettuce ... squashes, cucumber, melons, peas, beans, and other vegetables."

ANIMAL ENCOUNTERS

★ **New animals in the forests**

★ **Moose alert!**

The French hunted the beaver for its **pelt**, or fur, but they soon encountered other animals they had never seen. Moose and caribou lived all over the forests of New France and Acadia. Although moose live in northern Europe and Russia, Champlain and his men would not have seen them in France.

My Explorer Journal

★ **Champlain wrote accounts of what he had seen for King Henry IV. He saw many new animals and plants and described them in detail. If you had to write to the king, how would you describe a moose?**

> Ducks, bustards, grey and white geese, partridges, larks and other birds; moreover moose, caribou, otter, beaver, bear, wildcats, raccoons, and other animals."
> *Marc Lescarbot describes the wild animals at Port Royal.*

Foodstuff

Most settlers did not try native foods, such as corn, although some hunted native animals. Eventually, they shipped cattle from France to raise in New France.

Fortune Hunting

When they colonized New France, the French expanded their empire. Not only did they gain land, they also profited from the many riches the land had to offer.

Did you know?

The demand for fur grew because of fashions in the French capital, Paris. Many ship's captains and trappers broke the official monopoly on trading in furs.

Lots of Fish in this Sea

☛ **Fishing industry takes off**

☛ **Cod fever**

The French expanded their fishing industry into North America in the early 1500s. They fished off the coasts of Newfoundland and Labrador and found a rich supply of cod off the Grand Banks. Young and experienced fishermen alike traveled across the Atlantic Ocean in the early spring and fished until the fall. They salted the fish to preserve it during its long journey back to France.

PASSION FOR FUR

In the early 1600s, the felt hat became hugely popular in Europe, and the demand for beaver pelts soared. The trading posts were busy places where First Nations hunters brought furs to exchange for knives, pots, blankets, and other goods. In 1626, Cardinal Richelieu took command of New France and its fur trade. He established the Company of the Hundred Associates in order to expand trade and settle the land.

Explorers

The coureurs de bois led French exploration into the heart of Canada. They learned much geographical knowledge from their First Nations guides.

OUTLAW TRADERS

★ **Money to be made from fur**

★ **Adventurers head into the wilderness**

Some young French adventurers decided to hunt for fur themselves. These *coureurs de bois*, or "runners of the wood," did not work within the French laws. Instead, they lived with First Nations groups and learned many skills from the hunters. They lived in the wilderness for weeks or even months at a time.

COLONIAL BALANCE

★ **Foothold in North America**

New France was a useful French foothold in North America. France's traditional competitors, the English, were busy settling further south along the Atlantic coast. New France helped ensure that the English would not dominate the whole continent.

STAKING CLAIMS

☛ **Permanent settlements for France**

☛ **Priests spread Christian faith**

When Champlain founded Quebec, France finally had a permanent colony in the New World and a chance to further its empire. The money raised by the fur trade paid for hundreds of settlers to travel to New France. Jesuit priests also traveled to the new territories. They sought to convert the First Nations people to Christianity and to make them citizens of France.

This Isn't What It Said in the Brochure

Exploring a new frontier was thrilling. It was also full of danger, illness, and hard work. The new land presented problems at every turn, from bitter cold at St. Croix to attacks by native people.

PASS THE VITAMIN C

+ Go Suck on a Lemon

Scurvy is a disease caused by a lack of Vitamin C found in fresh fruit and vegetables. Half the settlers at St. Croix died of scurvy during the bitter winter of 1604–05. Champlain described their symptoms: "Their teeth barely held in their places, and could be drawn out with the fingers without causing pain."

BATTLE SCARS

- ☞ **Explorer suffers injury**
- ☞ **Bears a scar for life**

The battle against the Iroquois in 1610 was a victory for the French and their First Nations allies. In the battle, an arrow split Champlain's ear and lodged in his neck. A French surgeon treated the wounds, but Champlain had a scar for the rest of his life.

CONSPIRACY IN THE COLONY

★ Siege forces surrender

As Champlain started building his settlement in Quebec, he faced a serious problem. One of the men in his crew, Jean Duval, was plotting to kill him. Duval planned to sell the new settlement to the Spanish or Basques. Just in time, another man told Champlain of Duval's plan. Champlain arrested the conspirators, and Duval was hanged.

UNDER ATTACK

★ **Siege forces surrender**

★ **Settlers run short of provisions**

War broke out between France and England in 1627. King Charles I of England sent two French-born merchants, the Kirke brothers, to seize New France. After a failed attempt to take Quebec in 1628, they returned in 1629 and forced Champlain to surrender.

> " Louis Kirke … was French in disposition and always had a liking for the French nation."
> *Champlain describes Louis Kirke, to whom he surrendered Quebec.*

LOST IN THE WOODS

☛ **Three days in the wilderness**

☛ **Distracted by a beautiful bird**

Once when he was hunting with the Hurons, Champlain was distracted by a strange bird. It was "entirely yellow, except the head which was red, and the wings which were blue… The desire to kill it led me to pursue it from tree to tree…" Champlain became separated from his companions and was lost in the woods for three days before he found his way back to camp.

Did you know?

The Kirke brothers treated Champlain well, with one exception. They refused to allow him to take his adopted Montagnais daughters to France.

End of the Road

After spending most of his life traveling, Champlain settled in Quebec after France and England made peace. He helped to create the modern city.

ENGLISH CONTROL

- Illegal capture
- British forced to return Quebec

The winter of 1628–1629 was harsh, and the settlers were desperate for supplies to arrive from France. The hungry settlers could not fight the Kirke brothers, who were under orders to destroy Quebec. The Kirkes took Champlain as a prisoner to England. There, he learned that the war with France was already over. This meant that Quebec had been captured illegally, and so France reclaimed it.

KEY MAP!

In 1632, Champlain drew a map of New France that showed everywhere the French lived. The map was the basis of peace talks between the French and English.

> " Truly he led a life of great justice and equity, and with a perfect fidelity to his King and to the gentlemen of the Company"
> *Father Le Jeune on Champlain's death*

A LIFE'S WORK

★ Champlain publishes new book

Champlain wrote throughout his life. His first book, published in 1604, described the First Nations people he met. He called them "sauvages," meaning "forest dwellers." Three more books described his explorations in Acadia and New France. Champlain's writings were accompanied by many of his own drawings. Like his maps, the illustrations were detailed and well drawn.

A LEADER RETURNS

In 1633, Champlain finally had the chance to return to New France from Europe. The English had destroyed much of Quebec during their time there. Champlain began to rebuild his settlement. He repaired some structures and built new ones, including a chapel. He reconnected with the Montagnais and Huron people, and built a new trading fort at Trois-Rivières.

SETTLING IN FRANCE

☛ Come to New France!

☛ Workers needed!

In 1627, the Company of a Hundred Associates began to grant land rights in New France. They wanted to attract French settlers to the colony. Land still belonged to the king, but it was divided into long strips, called *seigneuries*. Farmers, called *habitants*, worked the land and paid taxes to the seigneur, or lord.

CHAMPLAIN'S LEGACY

+ Beloved leader dies at Quebec

Champlain led a busy life, but by fall 1635 he was growing tired. He suffered a stroke in October and died on December 25. The settlers and priests held a large funeral for him. Many First Nations people attended in order to say a final goodbye to a man who had become a loyal friend.

GLOSSARY

astrolabe An early navigational instrument used to measure the height of the Sun or other celestial bodies above the horizon

baptism A ceremony that uses water to proclaim someone to be Christian

barques Sailing ships with three or more masts

cartographer A person who studies and practices map drawing

colony A settlement or territory that is under the political control of a different country

cross-staff A navigational tool used to measure the angle of elevation of heavenly bodies

dialects Forms of a language spoken in a particular area

fertile Able to grow plants, including useful food crops, in great abundance

fidelity Being faithful or loyal

genealogist Someone who studies ancestry

latitude How far a location on Earth is north or south of the equator

Louvre A famous historical museum in Paris, France

monopoly Complete control over selling a particular type of commodity

patache A small sailing ship used mainly to carry men or cargo

pelt The skin of an animal with the fur or hair on it

pilot A sailor who steers a vessel, often in dangerous waters

port A city, town, or other place where ships load or unload goods

portage Carrying boats between two waterways or around an obstacle in a river; the path used is also called a portage

scurvy A disease caused by a lack of Vitamin C. Sufferers bleed under their skin and from their gums, and become extremely weak. Scurvy can be fatal.

seigneuries Areas of land farmed by settlers in New France on behalf of seigneurs, or noble landowners

shallop A small open boat with oars or a sail, or both, that holds about ten men and is used for traveling in shallow water

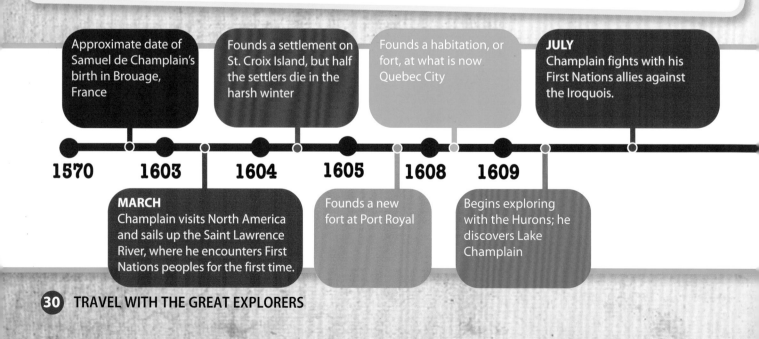

Approximate date of Samuel de Champlain's birth in Brouage, France

Founds a settlement on St. Croix Island, but half the settlers die in the harsh winter

Founds a habitation, or fort, at what is now Quebec City

JULY Champlain fights with his First Nations allies against the Iroquois.

1570 **1603** **1604** **1605** **1608** **1609**

MARCH Champlain visits North America and sails up the Saint Lawrence River, where he encounters First Nations peoples for the first time.

Founds a new fort at Port Royal

Begins exploring with the Hurons; he discovers Lake Champlain

ON THE WEB

www.timetoast.com/timelines/ samuel-de-champlain--5
Interactive timeline of Champlain's life and exploration

http://library.thinkquest.org/4034/ champlain.html
Thinkquest page on Champlain, with links

www.pbs.org/empireofthebay/ profiles/dechamplain.html
PBS page about Champlain to accompany the series *Empire of the Bay*

www.newadvent.org/cathen/ 03567a.htm
Account of Champlain's life and career from the online Catholic Encyclopedia

BOOKS

Faber, Harold. *Samuel de Champlain: Explorer of Canada* (Great Explorations). Benchmark Books, 2004.

Hurwicz, Claude. *Samuel de Champlain* (Famous Explorers). PowerKids Press, 2003.

Morganelli, Adrianna. *Samuel de Champlain: From New France to Cape Cod* (In the Footsteps of Explorers). Crabtree Publishing Company, 2005.

Pelleschi, Andrea. *Samuel de Champlain* (Jnr. Graphic Famous Explorers). PowerKids Press, 2013.

Sherman, Josepha. *Samuel de Champlain; Explorer of the Great Lakes Region and Founder of Quebec* (Library of Explorers and Exploration). Rosen Central, 2002.

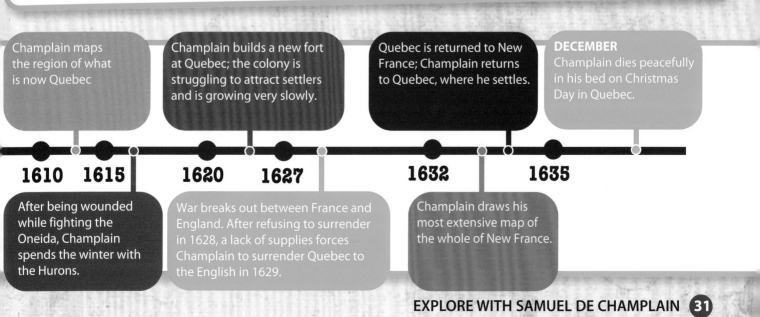

Champlain maps the region of what is now Quebec

Champlain builds a new fort at Quebec; the colony is struggling to attract settlers and is growing very slowly.

Quebec is returned to New France; Champlain returns to Quebec, where he settles.

DECEMBER Champlain dies peacefully in his bed on Christmas Day in Quebec.

1610   1615   1620   1627   1632   1635

After being wounded while fighting the Oneida, Champlain spends the winter with the Hurons.

War breaks out between France and England. After refusing to surrender in 1628, a lack of supplies forces Champlain to surrender Quebec to the English in 1629.

Champlain draws his most extensive map of the whole of New France.

INDEX